My Mom Is a TV News Anchor

As told to
Alan Trussell-Cullen

Dominie Press, Inc.

Publisher: Christine Yuen
Series Editors: Adria F. Klein & Alan Trussell-Cullen
Editor: Bob Rowland
Photographer: Simon Young
Designer: Gary Hamada

With thanks to: "One News," Television New Zealand, Liz Gunn (news anchor), and Margie Gunn.

Copyright ©2001 Dominie Press, Inc. All rights reserved. No part of this publication may be reproduced or transmitted in any form or by any means without permission in writing from the publisher. Reproduction of any part of this book, through photocopy, recording, or any electronic or mechanical retrieval system, without the written permission of the publisher, is an infringement of the copyright law.

Published by:

Dominie Press, Inc.

1949 Kellogg Avenue
Carlsbad, California 92008 USA

www.dominie.com

ISBN 0-7685-0610-7

Printed in Singapore by PH Productions Pte Ltd

2 3 4 5 6 PH 07 06 05 04

Table of Contents

What to Wear?	4
In the Makeup Room	6
Preparing the Broadcast	8
The News Script	10
At the News Desk	12
The News Begins!	14
Watching Mom Every Night	18
Picture Glossary	20
Index	20

Mm… What will I wear for the news tonight?

What to Wear?

My Mom is a TV news anchor.
This is her dressing room.
This is where her day begins.

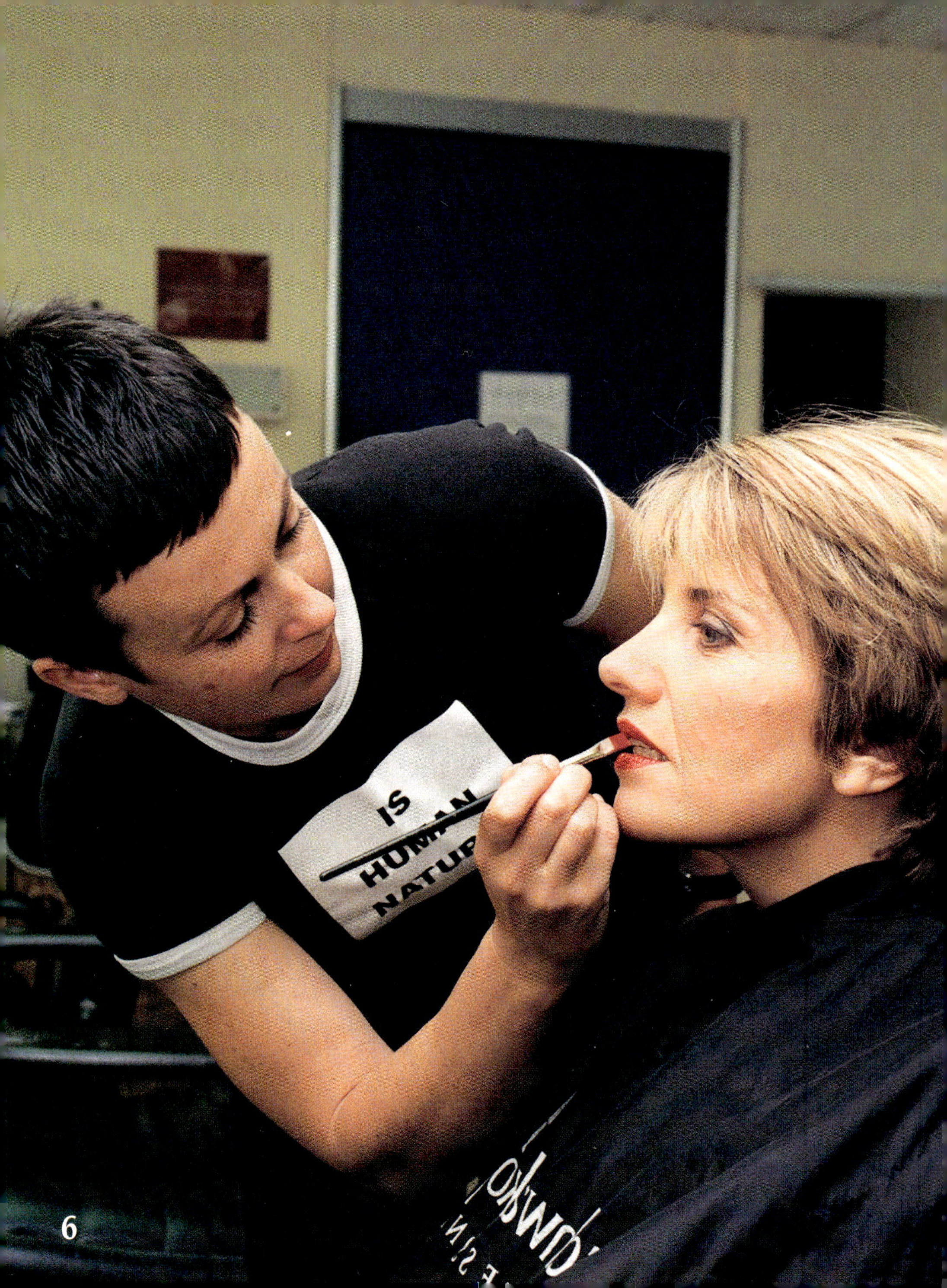
IS

In the Makeup Room

This is the makeup room. People on TV have to wear makeup because of the bright lights.

Mom has to wear special makeup on TV because of the bright lights.

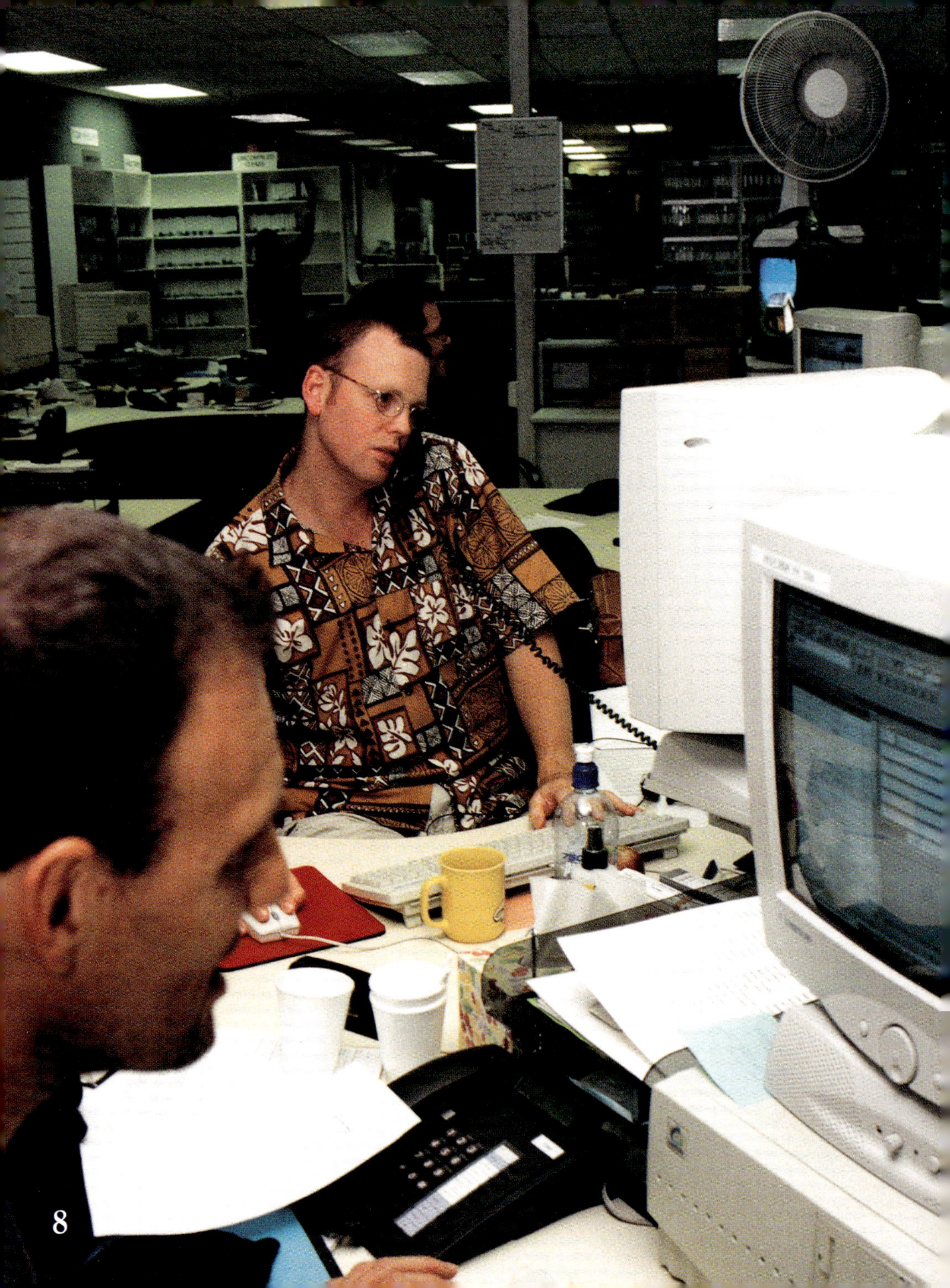

Preparing the Broadcast

This is the news room.

The news team writes the stories for Mom to read on TV.

What are the news stories for tonight?

The News Script

Now my Mom goes to her desk and checks the news stories for the TV news.

She reads them on the computer screen.

It looks good!

It sounds good!

12

At the News Desk

It is nearly time for the news on TV.

My Mom sits at the news desk in the TV studio.

One person checks the sound.
One person checks the camera.

Five, four, three, two, one... Roll News Intro!

The News Begins!

Lots of people help Mom do the news.

This is the control room. The director helps Mom start the news.

TelePrompTer

This is what my Mom sees
while she is reading the news.

She reads the news
from a special computer screen
she can see in front of her.

Watching Mom Every Night

And this is what I see
when I watch the news.

I am very lucky
because I get to watch my Mom
at work every night!

Picture Glossary

computer screen:

TelePrompTer:

makeup:

TV studio:

Index

camera, 13
computer screen, 11, 17
control room, 15

desk, 15
dressing room, 5

makeup room, 7

news desk, 13
news team, 9

sound, 13

TelePrompTer, 16
TV studio, 13